PLANT WISDOM

EVERYDAY SPIRITUAL PRACTICES WITH THE MOST COMMON ESSENTIAL OILS

by
Amber Jane Arquette

The information provided in this book is designed to provide helpful information on the subjects discussed. This book is not intended as a substitute for the medical advice of physicians. The reader assumes full responsibility for the application and results of the protocols and information in this book. In the event of a distress, please consult necessary health professionals. The author shall not be liable for any physical, psychological, or emotional damages including, but not limited to, special, incidental, consequential or other damages. The reader is responsible for their own choices, actions and results.

PRAISE FOR PLANT WISDOM:

I'm so in love with this book! I love the journey you take us on with every oil. They tell their own story, I feel like I'm on the journey with you while reading it. The information and understanding of the oils is priceless. I will definitely talk to and use my oils differently now. I love the book!! Amazing!!
   - **Stephanie Willis**

"Amber Jane is not only a modern day Medicine Woman, she's an incredibly gifted author. She has a brilliant talent for understanding and teaching the healing power of plants, and sharing in a way that is relatable and easily understood. You'll use this book a resource for your own healing, body, mind, and soul for many years to come."
   - **Rachel O'Rouke**

"Through her beautifully channeled messages in *Plant – A Spiritual Guide*, Amber Jane shows us a path to connect to the Plant Kingdom and to who we are at this very moment. We travel with her on her vivid journeys and "see" what gifts are waiting there for us. I appreciate the simplicity of the Living Rituals: such practical ways to create daily ceremonies that guide us to our hearts, our inner senses, and our power to heal. As I read the questions posed in each chapter, immediately the answers began rising up from within me. What a gift this book is, arriving at the perfect time to assist humanity to the truth of who we are. These benevolent messages are a celebration of our creative life as human beings. Thank you, Amber Jane!"

 - **Tracy McFarland**

DEDICATION

This book is dedicated to You, Dear one.

May the Wisdom of the Plants resonate inside you, waking up places in you that have been asleep long enough. May they remind you of your greatness, your beauty and your gifts. For we need ALL of you, now.

If you are reading this book, I believe your Soul came to the planet at this exciting time. There is no mistake, and in fact, you are a part of a most Divine Plan. You are needed right where you are, where you have been and where you are going. Your path is unfolding just as it should. I know that you have come here to make a difference. You have medicine for the people and for the Earth itself. You are a beacon of light—burn brighter, so that I can see you!

As I heal,
You heal.
As You heal,
I heal.
The ripples extend,
Across time and space and place.

CONTENTS

ACKNOWLEDGMENTS

We do not ever do it alone.

If it weren't for the support, love, belief, and listening of my miraculous friends and family this book would still be pages heavy on my heart.

Thank you to my dear friend, Judith Maxey, who shares the gift of hearing the voice of the Plant Kingdom. You have helped me feel sane and almost normal. You cheered me on from the very beginning, urging me to write and asking for this book to be born. I thank you for your encouragement and friendship. My Galactic sister, I love you. Let's grow old together.

April Hanson, my sweet friend. You may think that you leave a tender footprint in this world, but your tenderness has the fierce energy of the thundering hooves of a herd of Buffalo. I thank you for believing in my gifts and the goodness in my Soul. You have been so sure of me, helping me out of the low points to navigate this 3D reality. I hope we spend many more years witnessing each other step into greater and greater versions of ourselves.

My dear Mom, if it were not for your love, cheerleading, and acceptance I am not sure where I would be today. Thank you for your commitment to always bettering our relationship and for your articulated encouragement. Thank you for teaching me about family. And thank you for being an example of what it means to pursue growth and expansion, unendingly.

Justin Riede, you are far more than a husband and father to our daughter. You are my life partner, my best friend and my champion. You challenge me. You give me grace. You ask me to come down from the Stars and place both feet on the ground when needed. You love me through it all. You never lose hope. Thank you for accepting me "as is," for it has allowed me to grow. Thank you for listening to my tangents and "out there" stories without batting an eye. Thank you for your forgiveness and meeting me halfway. Thank you for reincarnating, yet again, with me. I am honored to hold your hand this entire lifetime, from 19 years of age to 109—at least!

Rose Ingraham, thank you for shining a light when my path was dark and I was lost. Thank you for showing me it was safe to come out of hiding. Most of all thank you for inspiring me to pursue the Plant Spirit Messages!

INTRODUCTION

Welcome.
My name is Amber Jane and I am a
galactic medicine woman
here to radiate healing across the globe.
But really, I'm my own human being
on a human being journey.

If, long ago, you were lucky enough to meet a medicine woman, she might have invited you in and pointed out a few of the jars she kept on her shelves. She might have mentioned their uses and described how her magical combinations heal different ailments and conditions.

But, one thing I promise you, she would *never* have shown you what was in her mysterious back room. And now, most of those ancient secrets are gone—they've been, buried, burned, lost or forgotten.

Some call me a modern-day medicine woman. I live in Portland, Oregon, with my daughter and husband, running an intuitive healing business, surrounded by trees on a quarter acre right in the middle of the city. It's peaceful and allows me to continue to live in this bustling town, in this fast paced modern world.

Why have I connected in so deeply with the Plant nation? Why me? Why Now? To start, I grew up in rural Northern California with my mom. Humboldt County – land of the Redwoods. She was an herbalist for many years and she used Plants for our daily medicine. From stomach aches to scarlet fever, it was the plants that remedied us. Because of this, I never created a familiarity with our modern day medical system. It was a way of life. I continued to use homeopathy and naturopathic medicine in my adulthood, leading me to confidently giving birth to my daughter naturally at our home. I believe this is part of why the Plants bring their messages to me. I believe in them. *Whole heartedly.*

Seven years ago doTERRA essential oils came into my life, through an Oil Fairy named Lotus Hartley. My first oil was a comforting blend for me and my baby. It was profound and also brought Ritual back into my daily life. I would rub the essential oil on my baby's feet every night before bed. I would start to chant my gratitude and tell her how amazing her body was. This was the start to my practice of "Living Ritual Daily". I immersed myself in learning everything I could about the plant oils. They were so similar to herbs; I felt a kinship right away. Then, I heard them. One day, after I had collected a good amount of oils, I had them all lined up on my shelf and I started to hear a kind of singing coming from them. It filled me with JOY. I felt the presence of Spirit behind these oils. I heard them calling me. I also felt them waking something deep inside of me. It was their first invitation to communicate. My Heart opened up to them with a resounding yes.

Now their song, their messages are in this book! I am proud and excited to open the door to my own back room. I believe it is time for us all to have access to *everything* we require for healing. Our world needs it so desperately.

Why now? Because it is time. We've been asking. We are ready. There was a time when plants and people spoke freely to each other. They came to our aid and we cultivated them in our back yards. Today, the plants are screaming at us to listen again. We have fallen out of relationship, from TV dinners to bottles of Aspirin. The truth is they are the equalizers for your overwhelmed cellular systems and your out of balanced emotional and energy bodies. They are the balm for your flourishing inflammation.

My process: Using a drumming technique and four years of training to access a Shamanic state of consciousness, I "journey" to the Plant Kingdom. I ask how they can help us in becoming the most true version of ourselves. How can we bring ritual and Spirit into our daily lives. How can they help us awaken to our own innate power. And how can they help us with the Ascension process. I am here to bring back Plant Wisdom into our homes by listening to them, telling their stories, and being their voice.

Dear reader, my deepest desire is for this book to have its own healing effect on you. As you read these personal messages from the Plant Kingdom let them fill your heart, touch your soul, and awaken your spirit. May your relationship with these Plant Allies deepen and grow. They have much wisdom to share. Their intention is to bring us back into relationship with ourselves as well as the natural cycles of the Earth itself.

Many blessings,

Amber Jane

HOW TO USE THIS BOOK

There are many creative ways you can use this book :

- Simply turn to a page, like picking an Oracle card. Ask the book for the perfect message to support you on your day.
- Read the book cover to cover to learn more about how dynamic your essential oils are.
- Work with one plant a week or a month. Keep a journal and track your experience.
- When you are feeling low, draw strength from the blessings at the start of each chapter.
- Use the index to find the feeling you are looking for. Or just simply read out loud all of the high vibration words in the index – fill the room with these frequencies.

My vision for this book is that you feel inspired to deepen your connection to the roots, trees, leaves and flowers, the Allies of the Plant Kingdom. That you invite Spirit in with the Living Ritual Daily section and receive a healing just by reading the words at the start of each chapter.

. . .

I begin each Plant Message with a blessing. It's my personal blessing to you from me. May this help open your Heart to receive the love that is always there for you in the natural world.

Next, I share with you some of the journey story I experienced when visiting the Plant. Then I deliver the specific message of the Plant, that leads into its message for you.

Each chapter has questions for you to ponder. As you read the question, be curious to see what your Soul reveals to you. There is no right answer. It's all about your connection to you. You can use these as journal prompts.

At the close of the chapter, I list Living Ritual Daily protocols on how to use these plant oils and blends. Perhaps you don't have the time in your busy day for a full-blown ritual, but with these Living Ritual Daily suggestions you will now have the power to make a sacred space for yourself, anytime and anywhere. I believe by simply pivoting our energy from routine to ritual we honor our Spirit and enrich our lives. The essential oils are a beautiful bridge to easily and intentionally bring ritual, meaning, love and connection into your day.

LAVENDER: THE OIL OF BLESSINGS

May the Blessing Fields open up and unburden this moment,
brightening your Heart Light so that it shines with radiance.
May deep listening allow you deeper connection.
May you allow your Heart to lead, blessed one.

Lavender's Message:

In my journey to Lavender, I see a stream of light descending from the Heavens, flowing into my Crown Chakra. A lotus flower forms. It is a beautiful, glowing purple, circling just above my head. As this pillar of light flows further into my body, it lights up my third-eye, allowing me to see with the eyes of Intuition. This light reaches down to my Heart center, giving my third-eye access to the wisdom of my heart, so that I can see with the eyes of love. This activation allows me to see with more clarity than the naked eye permits. This love shines from me. I feel safe, I feel peace.

While Lavender is the foundation of the medicine pouch and is used in many ways, it has been forgotten for one crucial ability. This Plant accesses and opens the Blessing Fields, connecting you to the Angelic realms. It illuminates and activates the crystal light within your own Heart so you can more easily send blessings to those who are strangers as well as those who are in relationship with you.

Call on the Angels to help in times of need. And call on Lavender to bless your way in the world and remind you that your Angels are always there for you. Ask your Angels to use their wings and clear away worries that weigh you down. Use the Oil of Blessings to do the same in ceremony as well as amplify your blessings upon those you cherish.

Lavender wants you to soften your view of others and see that they are doing the best they can and that there is goodness at the core of every-one. Also known as the Oil of Communication, Lavender tells me that in order to more deeply communicate you must first start with centering into the Heart, seeing the divine connection between you and them, and *then* listening in a new way by connecting into our higher consciousness. Lavender helps us to listen with genuine curios-ity, quieting mind chatter, clearing assumptions and releasing judgments.

Lavender helps you accept that others may have a truth that is different from yours, and it will help you feel that this is okay. It encourages you to pivot from victim and blaming mentality to percep-tions of connection and camaraderie. This Plant naturally guides you to speak with more thought and intention and to really listen in, inter-rupting your habit of automatic conclusions . This violet flower helps you choose words of alliance, curiosity, understanding and even forgiveness.

. . .

Lavender helps you to see from a larger vantage point of the situation at hand in place of the pin point of your pain. Lavender inspires *compassion*. With its high frequency, this oil lifts up your conversations and promotes honest heart-to-heart communication in place of exaggerated storytelling. It also helps to stop the habit of talking in circles and repeating old stories.

Lavender has an amazing ability to help us be comfortable with silence —teaching that sharing silence is a way to hear on a deeper level, to know someone in a different way. We often fill space with words because we are afraid of, or uncomfortable with, the intimacy that silence brings. With Lavender's assistance, you may naturally allow yourself to become vulnerable and transparent, authentic and honest. This may sound scary, but remember you are held by your Angels today as well as being soothed by Lavender.

Lavender promotes honesty. Ask the power of Lavender to clear the lies you have told yourself, the misperceptions you hold of others, and the need to exaggerate or fib in order to feel loved. With Lavender, you create new stories highlighting your own strengths, beauty, and talents, as well as new stories of others. This in itself is a blessing and brings out more of the goodness in them and in you.

Questions

If you were to ask for a blessing, right now, what would it be?
What lies have you been believing?
Which stories are habitually on repeat? Are you tired of telling them?
Who in your life might you see in a new light?

Living Ritual Daily

. . .

Use Lavender daily if you have trouble speaking your truth. With practice, you will rebuild trust in yourself that you are capable of graceful articulation and honesty. Blend with Geranium and place over your Heart and over your throat up towards your chin.

Anoint your throat with 1 drop of Lavender and 1 drop of Frankincense to find your singing voice. Sing to your dishes, to those in other cars as you drive, to the trees in the backyard. Open your throat so that the words in your heart can be expressed.

Diffuse or apply Lavender before or during crucial conversations. By activating the Blessing Fields in any exchange or sharing of words, you connect into greater possibilities. Partner with Rose to have heart to heart communication in relationship. Combine with Spearmint for speaking or presenting events. Combine with Sandalwood or Melissa to bring forth your Soul self.

Allow Lavender to clear the habit and culture of gossip. Do you want to change the way you talk about people or hear less gossip from a particular friend? Create a misting spray of Lavender, Clove and Wild Orange. In your morning ritual and before meeting your friend, mist around yourself. Amplify this magic by stating your intention or speaking a prayer out loud. The Angels are listening.

In challenging times, start your day with Lavender. Combine with Jasmine or Tangerine. Spend a moment seeing the Blessing Fields open, like a shaft of light to the Angelic realms. Your Angels are right by your side, helping you in miraculous ways. Keep asking for their intervention, support and love.

LEMON: THE OIL OF UNITY

May you feel energy, momentum, purpose and power building inside you.
May you tap into the divine consciousness of all moving parts.
May you be fluid from thought to action.
May you use the gift of collaboration to expand the joy of completion.

Lemon's Message:

My drumming takes me away to meet Lemon. I see the bright, rich color of yellow all around me. It energizes my senses and I feel if I reached out into it, I, too, would turn yellow. The color starts to fade. It becomes transparent, and, as if emerging out of a fog, I see a boat on a river.

A group of men row through muddy waters—they are paddling up the Nile River. Decorated with tribal art, their craft feels like a racing or a hunting boat. These men have rowed together many times. They have familiarity, fluidity and knowing.

Their skin is dark chocolate, their eyes trained on the water, reading things that we do not see. Their bodies move as one, and they silently listen to the heartbeat of one another and the life around them. They are practiced at working with the elements and intimately know the water, the sun, the wind, and the wood of the boat. They are fast and precise as they work together, faster than any one of them could be alone. Their individual skills outbalance any weaknesses. They have lost the need to be "ME," and are rewarded as the masterful "WE."

Lemon asks you to learn from these men as they unwaveringly work together to reach their goals and accomplish their tasks. Lemon helps you learn and integrate their focused, skillful ways by showing that collaboration is more powerful than individual accomplishment. It calls you to surrender individual gain for the abundance the whole can bring—where no one questions *how* to reach the goal because all know that reaching it is inevitable.

Clear distractions and deepen commitment to your goal. Lemon ignites determination from the inside out. It brings in a pure and potent energy, fuel, and focus that is unattached to anything outside the goal. The energy of Lemon helps you synchronize all the parts, aspects and details of a task and carries you across the finish line.

Lemon inspires you to trust. Usually people feel it's necessary to "earn" trust. Lemon tells us, *"Don't waste your precious time and energy holding back Trust."* It's like a dam holding water. Take down the dam, and allow the flow. Trust Spirit, trust others, trust yourself and take a Leap of Faith.

You have been taught to be cautious and closed, and now is the time to open. You are ready, you have matured, you can use your improved awareness and elevated level of consciousness to steward and create in a good way. Planet Earth is calling you, and Lemon will help you rise to the occasion.

It's also time to explore new levels of intimacy. It is safe now. Hurts don't have to be so hurtful; they can simply be bumps and scrapes from which you move on as you keep your eye on what's most important. Take things less personally. This essential oil asks you to get up, dust off and keep moving.

Lean on Lemon for motivation and rejuvenation. The magic of this citrus from Sicily is its ability to clear the blocks in front of you. The more you practice having clear intentions and aligned goals, the more swiftly you will reach your targets. Allow Lemon to remove distractions and help you enter the focused space of "nothing else matters." You are capable, engaged, you have inner peace and keen focus. You are un-distractible.

This Fruit fills you with endless confidence and inspires a faith beyond explanation. Lemon tells us that *"Together WE are the answer."*

Questions

In what ways do you fear surrendering yourself to the whole?
What are you afraid of losing if you do?
What part of you is out of sync?
What does Alignment feel like?

Living Ritual Daily:

Add Lemon to your water daily. Lemon can help you walk through life more intentionally. With every drop, use Lemon to create an intention for the next segment of the day. Call in more ease, safety, laughter or focus, for example.

Diffuse 3 drops each Lemon and Bergamot and 2 drops Rosemary to encourage collaboration and security in a new group or team.

A mix of Lemon and Digestive Blend will help synchronize you from the inside out, claim your strength, and live on purpose. Diffuse during a meditation; apply over your liver or on the bottoms of your feet.

Create an *Alignment* blend: 3 drops Lemon, 1 drop Helichrysum, 2 drops Rose, 1 drop Frankincense and 1 drop Sandalwood. Use this blend to come into more Alignment in your life. Ask to be reminded to reserve your "Yes" for what is true for you.

PEPPERMINT: THE OIL OF RELEASE

May you allow what is rising to the surface to be released.
May your true self come out of hiding.
May you embody neutrality.
May you find that there are treasures hidden in your pain.

Peppermint's Message:

As I drum, Peppermint sores in, in the form of Dragon, fierce, strong and giant. It is guiding me, like the North Star, sparkling blue and white, leading me to my Healing Helpers and Benevolent Ones. Peppermint wears a playful grin that soothes my worry and gives my protective Ego a rest.

Peppermint's cool breath blows away my attachments to false identities and any of my overly egoic embellished storylines. I remember that as I release I become a Hollow Bone, a clear channel, for Divine Wisdom and the truth of myself. If all I did in life was channel my true self, dear Ego, that would be enough for I am enough. Peppermint whispers to my Ego, *"Let go and rest, old friend."* And whispers to me, *"Let your healing story come forward. Remember your brilliance."* I feel a surge of energy as I come out from hiding.

Peppermint wants you to know its immense ability to activate healing energies and clear whatever is rising to the surface to be healed. It gives you new perspectives on emotions, experiences and situations, and eases the pain that your expectations have caused. This Oil of Release opens the channels for life force energy to come through and transform these dense, "negative" feelings and low-vibrations.

Peppermint is your North Star, brightly illuminating your way. This Plant points you in the right direction, and unravels what is tied up and needs to be freed. By helping connect you to your Guides, it helps navigate the way for your greatest self to emerge to a life that is full-filling.

The Archangels love to float in on the frequency of Peppermint. Their quiet gentility contrasts with the piercing aroma of this bold essential oil, but their aid is pungently powerful in the likeness of Peppermint.

Peppermint invites you to let go of the unnecessary details—all the *this and thats of life*—because under the flog is the truth you are seeking. It supports you in letting go of the stipulations, the distracting dramas, the long-windedness of what happened to whom, and the rights and wrongs of any situation. After all, these are just the Ego's points of reference. Let your attachment to what no longer serves you melt away with ease.

．．．

This essential oil fills your lungs, frees your narrow perspective, and blows away what is clouding your awareness, whether that be from emotions, pain or judgment. It brings ease into what is happening now, all the while providing a protective halo from the chaos around you. You can stay clear-headed, peaceful, and unharmed. Peppermint helps you center in your truth, unbending to another's will.

Peppermint can also connect you to the astrological constellations and support your efforts in translating the Stars. Using this Plant, you can begin to decipher the deeper wisdom and immense guidance of these unseen celestial influences with a clear view.

This meadow plant, bright-green and fresh-scented, reminds you to move in a more refined way in the world by anchoring in neutrality. Peppermint teaches the difference between force and flow. It encourages you to be like water, which is both neutral *and* powerful. Water does not force itself upon another, yet it dissolves obstacles and maneuvers around blockades. It is always accepting nature's agenda and surrendering to the journey, while carving out its own effortless way.

Peppermint invites you into a state of contentment and self-love, no matter what is present. In this culture, you are constantly taught to want more, strive for more and super-size your life. This focus can blind you to the moments of sweet contentment, enough-ness and presents which give space for gratitude to thirve.

When you are unattached to the how and surrender to the mystery of life, the Universe has an opportunity to lead you to the doorstep of your dreams and desires. You become open to new possibilities. As you release you make room for the new. With Peppermint's power, clear the layers of a lifetime of stories from your canvas. Paint a new picture of the joy you want to feel.

Questions:

What is rising to be released/healed?
What can be cleared so you can see the truth of the matter?
What would it take for your true self to play more full-out?
What does neutrality feel like?

Living Ritual Daily

In challenging times when you need to clear the chaos, create a blend of 5 drops of Peppermint and 3 drops of Petitgrain in a 2-ounce misting bottle. Spray around your body throughout the day.

Use 1-2 drops of this essential oil aromatically or topically before giving or receiving guidance of any kind: astrology or card readings, mentor or coaching calls or healing sessions or massage. Especially useful for practitioners.

In meditation, place a drop of Peppermint on your forehead and the roof of your mouth; Lie back and get lost in the astral pictorials of the starry sky. Soak in the starlight and the love that beams down from the heavens. Allow it to penetrate deep into your body and mind. As it invigorates, Peppermint awakens the Star Seeds still sleeping inside you.

. . .

Rub Peppermint and Wintergreen into the shoulders as you ask the Archangels to lift your burdens and work their magic.

MASSAGE BLEND: THE OIL
OF DANCE

May you find the dance of your Soul; May you hear the music of your Heart.
May you jump, shake, and twirl until your heaviness falls away.
May vitality inspire your every day as you become the
joyful blazer of your own beautiful trail.

Massage Blend's Message

I journey, and I hear shaking rattles and pounding drumbeats all around me. I feel bodies bumping into me. As my eyes clear, I see ecstatic faces full of joy. It's like a storm of pure elated motion, as these beings swirl and twirl to the music of their hearts' songs. Vitality. Power. Freedom. I am swept away into my own heartbeat, and fueled with ancient life-force energy.

I see in this moment that life can be so much more fun than we have been taught. The joyous celebration reminds me how much I gain by dancing my body through life, following the beat of my own drum and mastering my own instrument.

As I listen to the music and my body moves to its own rhythm, a newfound abandon sweeps over me. I feel a deep, long-submerged energy pulse alive, flowing to the surface.

In a symphony, one instrument does not create the beauty. It takes all the sounds, together, to make music that vibrates into the Soul's fabric.

The Spirit of this blend asks, "Why would you ever want to be the same as someone else? Are you not here to create or co-create a magnificent masterpiece with your own talents?" Massage Blend helps you hear your own drumbeat and contribute your unique notes to the universal anthem.

This essential oil asks you to move your body, reminding you that dance is a part of being alive. When the physical body is more flexible, the mind and spirit can enter more easily, and open you to the energy of new outcomes, solutions and formations. Moving your body breaks the shackles of fear.

Life is mysterious, unexpected, and always changing. So often we hang on too tightly. Massage Blend gives you the tools to move with the flux and flow of life, loosening your rigid grip. This enlivening blend of Plant oils invites you to dance to your own rhythm and helps you build the strength and agility to meet any circumstance.

Massage Blend also offers resilience. Imagine walking up a mountain, step by step. You feel bold and in your purpose as you walk. You have surrendered to the process and the conclusion. You cry out, brave and strong, "Yes, I can!" even when you're at your edge. That's because you are using and engaging your whole self. You remain devoted and zealous—and up the side of the mountain you go.

At the summit you lift your head, and see brilliance all around. You stop for a moment to take in the view, pure and expansive. You feel the aliveness of the Universe pour into you. Bliss. Wonder. Gratitude. Your capacity to accomplish more than you ever believed you could just expanded a thousand-fold.

Allow your Heart to beat in such celebration more often. This Blend helps you feel the dance rolling up your body from your feet to your knees, through your pelvic bowl, and out to your limbs. The dance and this energy are alive in you. You are enchanted as your whole spirit praises life, says yes again, and embodies resilience, inner peace and joy.

When we are committed to our own heartbeat, we are less concerned with the path that others are taking. We can hear the music of our soul and comparison melts away. Don't focus on what others are doing. Remember, you have your own instrument to play.

Questions

Where have cobwebs grown because you have not moved your body in so long?
What would it take for you to find your own rhythm?
What would change if you danced to the beat of your own drum?

Living Ritual Daily

. . .

Use Massage Blend to release and shake off any energy that does not match you. Put this oil into the diffuser or on the bottoms of your feet, turn on inspiring music, and dance yourself into center, into your divine expression. Dance frees your spirit and grounds you into your body, giving your mind a rest.

Use this Blend to inspire movement. If you have wanted to have more movement and exercise in your life, it will support you. Apply before and during warm-up.

Massage Blend is helpful when you have lost your way and forgotten what is important to you. It helps you increase faith and trust in your body and your belief in "I can!" Blend a drop each of Massage Blend and Sweet Fennel and apply to your temples, wrist creases and over your heart.

BREATHING BLEND: THE OIL OF RECEIVING

May breath fill your lungs, stretching and
growing your capacity to receive.
May it easily clear stuck emotions and release that which does not serve.
May each breath be more mindful than the last.
May your expansion be full of grace.

Breathing Blend's Message

In my journey, I am greeted by a short, smiling, cinnamon-skinned Native woman. She reaches out a soft, weathered hand and leads me into a glowing cornsilk-colored teepee, slightly hurrying me in her excitement. Under my bare feet, the ground inside is well worn, like her hands. She speaks about my Spirit body, and the freedom I have forgotten. She invites me to remember.

So it begins, the message of these Plants.

. . .

I can go anywhere, she tells me with a twinkle in her eye. I can close my eyes, open my mind and let my Spirit body roam. And I do—I close my eyes and relax. I feel light... lighter, weightless. I feel free. I am flying above the landscape, looking down upon the lush Earth. A bright delight flows through my body—I am remembering the beauty and spaciousness of this Spirit form.

Breathing Blend urges you to take a trip outside of your limited physical reality—whether through meditation, astral-travel, trance or daydream. In the physical world, which you're taught is all there is, your human reality easily forgets the infinite possibilities you have access to. When you live without connecting to your Spirit self, you constrict your reality, imagination, dream life and intuition. But when you allow your Spirit to travel, it returns to you with renewed belief in possibilities, freedom, perspectives and solutions.

You are a creator, and this essential oil blend connects you to the vast supply of creation energy—the clay ready to give form to your ideas, dreams and inspirations—which is limited only by the scope of your imagination.

Consider your breath. It rises and falls naturally. Your lungs expand and receive. Breath is your first gift of life and your last. It keeps you alive and keeps all of your systems working, yet you often don't notice it. Your breath connects the present moment with your multidimensional self. Following your breath in meditation is like opening the windows and letting fresh air flow into a stale room. Even 10 minutes heightens your brain activity, oxygenates your body and opens your ability to receive.

. . .

Take note! Your capacity to serve is proportional to your capacity to receive. If you wish to serve the world, you must also be versed in accepting the gifts of others, as well as asking and allowing for help. After all, your lungs must be full before you can exhale. Just as the cup must also be full in order to give.

The Universe is always working on your behalf. It is always seeking the most direct way to materialize your desires and guide you to where you want to be. Yet your mind can be like a maze that energy has to maneuver through. This Plant combination helps lower the walls of the maze, making it a powerful Ally in manifesting.

Mother Nature is always offering itself. This fresh, bright and herbaceous blend reminds you that you are not alone. This blend aids in clearing the way as you project your visions, intentions and prayers out to the world. Use this Breathing Blend to build on your relationship with the higher power you believe in. Practice handing over the "How" and the need to figure it out. And know that your job is to follow what lights you up.

The body houses just a fraction of your HUGE Spirit self. This essential oil encourages you to be loving towards the body and to say, "Thank You" for all it does, even when you are not watching. When you greet your body with Gratitude, it strengthens access and opens to the energy and wisdom of the bigger version of YOU.

Questions:

In what ways, in what places or around what people do you constrict your breath? Are you afraid? Are you unworthy?
How can you practice accepting more gifts, compliments and help?

What would it take to expand your capacity to (fill in the blank) more than you're able to now?

Living Ritual Daily

Open up to receive! Start your day with this morning routine to expand your container. Diffuse 2 drops Breathing Blend, 1 drop Litsea, and 2 drops Wild Orange. Journal or meditate on the feelings you want to feel this day. Breathe in and fill your lungs with these feelings.

Connect in with the Universe, God, Spirit (or whatever name you use) by placing 1 drop each Breathing Blend and Melissa on your third-eye, Heart Chakra and the back of your neck. Close your eyes and ask to feel its presence in your life. Ask for it to give you a specific sign throughout the day that it is with you, supporting and loving you.

Use this blend to expand your capacity to receive: 6 drops Shielding Blend, 8 drops Spearmint, 4 drops Tangerine, 4 drops of Wild Orange. Place in a 10ml roller bottle and fill with fractionated coconut oil.

DIGESTIVE BLEND: THE OIL OF PURPOSE

May you dissolve what does not serve you.
May your inner voice speak more clearly and reveal your truth.
May you trust that the path you are walking is yours.
May you feel at peace with divine timing.

Digestive Blend's Message

This journey takes me to a landscape of rolling hills and vibrant green open pastures. The sky is grey and cloudy, and has been this way for centuries. I feel a cold wind on my skin, and the nutrient-rich earth beneath my feet. This land both nurtures me with its stark beauty and exposes me to the elements of air, rock and water as I walk alone.

It asks me to find my own way, as does this oil blend. Can I make peace with the elements, like the animals who live here? Some part of them knows the harsh elements give them the sweetest grass to graze upon.

. . .

A light rain falls on my face, purifying my body, mind and spirit. The combination of these essential oils will do the same. I feel lighter, calm and cared for. Unburdened.

These Plants come together to wash away your resistance to life's natural unfolding, and help reveal your purpose. They do this by literally "digesting" and "dissolving" all you have been fed that is not the truth of who you are.

Digestive Blend helps you surrender into the process of releasing your burdens, especially the ones that are not yours. It gives perseverance and patience while you wait for things to shuffle into place and unfold in divine timing. The message of this savory blend: *Slow down and find what there is to appreciate in each stretch of life. Don't miss out on treasures by speeding through time.*

You are in a *life's* work, not a season of it. Digestive Blend wants you to trust and accept what is right now, and summon patience while waiting for the divine plan to unfold.

Digestive Blend knows that taking courageous action is part of the medicine you need in order to live in your truth, and it helps you to do so. Especially when your truth looks different from another's or from your upbringing. In those times when the world doesn't agree with you, Digestive Blend does. It's that wise voice inside you, urging you to take the steps that will lead to your purpose.

So many aspects of your life and body are working hard on your behalf.

This blend helps heal, nurture and soothe all these pieces in motion. On a physical level, this essential oil supports healthy digestion of your food. When you consider how you take in information daily and how your mind digests the outside world, you can understand just how much this blend does for you on the mental, spiritual and energetic levels.

If you are trying to break a habit, whether it's ignoring your intuitive hunches or staying up until 1 a.m., Digestive Blend will break down your resistance to change. This savory blend reminds us that the Universe knows the easiest way to our heart's desires. What you might see as a detour might be the way to pick up new and needed skills, strengths, and tools for the next chapter ahead. Digestive Blend says, *"You are constantly building the version of yourself that already has everything you want."*

Questions:

What inner suggestions have you been ignoring?
What step or courageous action can you say "Yes" to today?
What would you ask Digestive Blend to dissolve?

Living Ritual Daily

If you are feeling lost, use this oil in meditation by diffusing or rubbing below the navel. Apply before a journaling session to reveal your quieted inner voice. Allow your thoughts and words to flow—this practice is like the rain washing away the chaos to get to the calm truth within.

. . .

Ask for your purpose and path to be *gracefully* reveled to you. Combine Digestive Blend with Frankincense and/or Rose, dilute with carrier oil. Each morning for 7-14 days, anoint the bottoms of your feet and the base of your spine.

This oil blend works on so many levels and is wonderfully supportive for times of personal change and challenge. Diffuse Digestive Blend to inspire more courage and turn around any victim mentality that's limiting you.

PROTECTIVE BLEND: OIL OF THE LEGION OF KINGS

May you feel the strength of an army walking behind you.
May you be courageous and sovereign with each step you take.
May you feel your own greatness amplified.
May you treat yourself well, because you are worth fighting for.

Protective Blend's Message

Like a scene from *The Lord of the Rings*, I see a King, strong and full of certainty, faith and power. Light shines from behind him. As I look closer, I see he is backed by a vast army. He has never lost a battle, and has no reference for how such a loss would feel. Though he is strong, mighty, undefeatable, I recognize that he is also good-hearted, and brings that goodness and integrity to the World. He has come to us to fight for our honor, our protection, and our wellbeing.

This blend invites us to tap into a Legion of Kings and have access to an arsenal of power used by many a skilled and valiant hero. It hands over a rich and royal lineage, one that has won every challenge it has ever met. And it will ensure such victory is at the end of our stories, too.

When anointing this essential oil blend, it is as if a gleaming, shimmering suit of armor envelops the body. A golden light of exuberant vitality beams all around. Ornate decorations covering this armor bring the beauty and seal of the Plant Kingdom, which reminds us how the Plants endlessly protect our physical and energetic bodies. We feel a deep faith that the goodness welling up inside us will prevail. We are safe and protected, lifted up and out of the mundane and into the gallant energies of victory.

Protective Blend reminds you that your heart is pure. It will align you with your integrity and inspire you to act with honor and respect versus acting from revenge, "an eye for an eye," or responding in kind. This essential oil blend has an allegiance to your wellbeing. It urges you to respect and honor your physical body as well, by inspiring you to build up strength, agility, flexibility, wellness, and rest.

This Plant Ally also helps deflect the drama of other people that can influence your life, and inoculates you against the mental and physical spread of this type of "infection." When using Protective Blend, you may find the way drama sounds or feels to be undesirable. You might find yourself ending a conversation or walking away with nothing to say, in place of leaning in with interest as you used to. It is just not a match for you anymore.

Protective Blend pulls you out of the trenches of life by empowering you and giving you the spark to get up and try, and try again. You are headed for a good ending. Believe. Inspired by the zesty aroma of trees, citrus and spices, you will not forget that all is working in your favor. It may take everything you have to turn things around but you have Protective Blend on your side. It is possible.

No matter what seems "broken," this Plant magic is here to show you that *it is* fixable. Whether it takes a week or a year, you will be standing at the edge of your kingdom in a victorious new reality.

Questions

In what ways can you align yourself to your optimal wellbeing?
What does your Kingdom look like? What is it known for?
If you believed in yourself the way these Kings do, what actions would you take, what would you do?

Living Ritual Daily

Protective Blend brings out the divine power of balanced masculinity. If you are feeling unbalanced in this area—for example, too dominating or unable to listen with neutral ears—roll a diluted version, 1 drop of Protective blend and 1 drop of Patchouli over your lower belly and/or your lower back and heart Chakra daily. This will help you move into action with grace when needed or asked, instead of searching the horizon for people in distress or jumping to a solution too quickly.

When you feel uncertain, this essential oil can guide you away from that which is not a divine match for you. Use it purposefully by asking these Plants to help you pivot your thoughts from what you don't want to what you do want. Combine with Melissa to amplify your greatness. Anoint or diffuse.

Protect yourself from the drama of others with this blend: 5 drops Protective blend, 3 drops Frankincense, 1 drop Pink Pepper and 1 drop Black Pepper in a 5ml roller bottle, fill with carrier oil. Or diffuse it when drama is present so you can get to the core of the issue.

Protective Blend is also known for its Abundance properties. It will help you manifest, simply by magnetizing what you desire to you. Use this essential oil in your Abundance rituals or anoint your notebook of

"Dreams & Desires," your gratitude journal, or a letter to the future. You can also put a drop in your hand as you say your daily affirmations aloud.

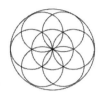

MELALEUCA: THE OIL OF PURITY

May you remember your divine beauty.
May you attract more of those who celebrate your truth.
May you learn discernment with ease.
May you feel sovereign and clear.
May a weight be lifted as you read these words.

Melaleuca's Message:

I am sliding into a sticky, tar-like mud. Sinking, oozing in. First my legs are trapped, then my torso. I can't move—it's too heavy and too thick. It is circling my neck. My head slowly descends into the gooey darkness. I am engulfed.

All I see is the darkness around me and hear nothing but silence. I feel alone and disconnected, my senses numbed, my awareness muted.

At times, life feels like this mud. You get stuck and weighed down by the untruths you have been told and now are living. The numbness and darkness builds up. But there is hope beyond these false beliefs, false actions and false roles. Melaleuca gives you the opening your soul has been yearning for. It's the chance to wash away the muck and residue accumulated over all these years.

Melaleuca extends its hand down into the mud and pulls you out. With its immense strength, it easily carries you to the pond at the foot of the ancient Melaleuca tree. The waters rinse away the mud off your body, skin, eyes, and heart. The untruths transmute with this infused crystal-clear water. You are bathed back to your purest form.

This essential oil connects you to your inner knowing, your values, your integrity and your sovereignty—the knowing of what it is like to be the purest version of you. The magic of this Plant literally dissolves away the gooey layers of influences from the World. This magnificent tree unhooks you from cultural insanity, pulling back your personal life-force energy from the false realities of others.

Unlock your inner kingdom with this essential oil. Melaleuca reaches down to dark places within you that have been forgotten or hidden. No matter how disconnected you may have become and no matter what secrets you've been keeping—even from yourself—it can help you go deep to retrieve the gifts you were born with.

We all unfold in our own timing. Melaleuca reminds you to respect your own pace of awakening. This Plant Ally activates a force field around you, an energetic barrier of protection, if you ask. Stand in this radiant, peaceful safety. Allow in only the energies of the true self—or greater.

· · ·

Melaleuca is adept at clearing cords and purifying wounds. This essential oil is a tonic that brings the flawless state of being to the present. Melaleuca encourages those who can't celebrate your divine beauty to effortlessly fall away from your life, as it dissolves the cords that have tied you to situations that are not for highest good.

Melaleuca also inspires you to safeguard your energy. You may find it unsettling to feel less worry and pity for others' pain, but know that this is good. Others do better when you see their brilliance and reflect that back to them with compassion instead of sympathy.

Melaleuca says, *"With your pure heart, pure mind, and hands clear and clean, walk in the direction your inner compass is leading you. Take your next step in the world with authority and a deeper sense of self."*

Questions:

Where will your inner compass lead you now?
What truth of you are you remembering? What lie are you releasing?
What secrets have you been keeping from yourself?
What kind of freedom comes with sovereignty?

Living Ritual Daily

Visualize Melaleuca offering you a branch from the Melaleuca tree. Shake the branch full of leaves around your body like a rattle, rattling off any stuck energy. Break up false identities that have formed in you. Knock off worries that have weighed you down. Spray or mist Melaleuca around your body and auric field. See these old, unneeded energies fall to the ground. Misting spray: 1 oz bottle with 7 drops of Melaleuca, add one of your favorite essential oils to enhance the aroma.

Clear out your ears! Have you heard untruths about yourself or others? Dab a few drops of diluted Melaleuca around the ear to clear out gossip or misperceptions about who you really are. Purify the vibrations of these words that may still echo in your mind. Apply this essential oil daily until you remember your truth or the truth of another.

Use Melaleuca as a Shaman's Mirror or a Wizard's Shield. Apply topically or mist around your body. Place a drop on a diffuser necklace and ask this essential oil to work for you. Blend 3 drops each Melaleuca, Lavender and Shielding blend.

SOOTHING BLEND: THE OIL OF HOPE

May you awaken to your Star Seed origins.
May hope color your thoughts.
May joy, freedom, the frequencies of the fifth dimension,
move through your every cell in your body.
May you feel the support of a Galaxy of beings who love you.

Soothing Blend's Message:

In my journey, I find myself swimming in a pool of stars, sky and space. I'm enveloped in a silken black liquid full of luminous, floating white lights twinkling all around me. The stars tickle my toes as I move—they sink and then come bobbing back to the surface. They fill me with curiosity and playfulness.

I notice that I, too, am full of Stars. I am made of Stardust. I am a Star child. I am here on Earth to be a beacon of light. I came with the ability to transmit a higher frequency of love, and a penetrating hope. And so did YOU.

Our physical body needs our spiritual body—and vice versa. We cannot function on Earth without both. Soothing Blend helps soften the physical symptoms that come with ascension, such as unusual aches, anxiousness, heart palpitations and a longing for Home. More of us than ever are holding new energies, thoughts and ideas. This can be draining and your body might feel heavier than before. You may be at a loss for words and experiencing the higher frequencies irritating your endocrine system with sleep interruption or hormone imbalances. Soothing Blend helps anchor these incoming energies with more comfort and ease.

Most of you reading this book have felt misunderstood and even abandoned by the third-dimension way of living and thinking on this planet. Maybe you feel like an alien in the crowd. Soothing Blend reassures you that your natural way of being is *valuable* and you are in the right place. You have just been two or three steps ahead—and now is the time for the world to catch up to *you*.

These Plants are asking you to listen and act on your natural inclinations, and to continue living with your Heart open. This blend will help you break the habit of altering who you truly are to fit in, for you're an important example for those around you. Authenticity is key.

Your Galactic tribe of sisters and brothers is here for you. When times are dark and being in a human body is tiring, this reassuring blue essential oil blend helps you draw on their unwavering support, hope, and vitality. Soothing Blend knows that the future is bright, brighter than the most radiant star in the sky.

. . .

This blend also helps you find other Star Seeds like yourself. As more of us turn up our Light, the easier it is for us to see each other, to connect and help all of us ascend. But as we become a brighter and bigger broadcast of Light, like a radio tower standing tall, we can become wary or worried. Soothing Blend offers strength and comfort as you raise your head to be seen and heard. It relieves any parts of your body that are challenged in your expansion.

This essential oil blend tells me there is more goodness and change, healing and happiness on the planet than ever before. There *is* more love and awakening than you know. Be assured.

You are the one you have been waiting for and all of the Galactic families are smiling down at you. They're amazed and in awe as you deconstruct your ego, heal your wounds, lead from your heart, use your gifts, forgive and hold the vision of a New World.

Soothing Blend folds you into the momentum of the change you are seeking. It says, *"You are doing the work and there are enough like you on the planet, changing the old into the new. It is happening faster than you think."*

Questions:

What fuels you? Do more of that!
Who or what is distracting you from your natural state of being?
How can you remind yourself of the light you have come to broadcast?

53

Living Ritual Daily

When you feel the heaviness of life, the force of swimming against the current, and the chaos of lower frequencies, turn to Soothing Blend. Rub a few drops into the parts of your body that are tired, usually the shoulders. Find rejuvenation and allow yourself to reconnect to those energies that fuel you.

Anoint this essential oil on the spine to activate your Star origins and help you find more like-minded people. Apply on your temples before any type of social gathering and intentionally ask to meet another Star Seed. Soothing Blend will show you that you are not alone.

Diffuse with Frankincense and allow it to penetrate your Body, Mind and Spirit. Melt into its embrace. Breathe in hope, breathe out peace.

Take a moment in your morning practice or during the day. Put one drop of Soothing Blend on top of your head. See yourself as a beacon of light. Start to Om, tune or hum. Visualize light radiating out of you, like sound waves, to life all around you.

FRANKINCENSE: THE OIL OF SOURCE ENERGY

May you embody your brilliance and
feel a warm glow fill your every corner.
May your mind return you to the peaceful moment of now.
May you remember you are a child of the Universe
and open to the adoration that is here for you.

Frankincense's Message:

In my journey, an image of a whisk broom sweeps into my mind. My thoughts are swirling in a spiral of thoughts, ideas, memories and to-dos. I feel dizzy and can't think straight. And then, just like it has come, the chaos is gone. Frankincense has cleared away all of it, leaving my mind still and peaceful.

In this journey to Frankincense, I enter a hot, barren landscape. The Sun blazes relentlessly, and there is no water, nor even a hint of a breeze. Here the scraggly Frankincense tree stands on hard rock, its gnarly roots grasping like a claw to the side of a cliff. It overlooks a vast view of dusty, sunburnt orange—a land where very little can survive. And yet here thrives a tree of greatness—a symbol of eternal health—a pillar of strength, wisdom, and connection to the Divine.

Frankincense grows amidst harsh elements in a tiny region of the world. What a metaphor for our human experience, in which the most powerful versions of ourselves are created in the most unlikely circumstances. Without challenging times, we would not access the deep inner strength that each human is born with. The strength of Source.

And so, Frankincense unites you with Source. It pours from the Heavens into your consciousness and your body. Cascading down and anchoring in. It grounds you in your truth, activates your gifts and heightens your strength. Frankincense says: *"You are a child of God, ever held in this caring light. This will get you through anything."*

This essential oil reminds us that when we simply rely on our human selves and the physical realm, it's like trying to walk with only one foot. We need both our feet to walk with agility and speed. Just as we need our Source connection to truly exist in full expression.

This warm and luminous oil reminds you that you do not need anything from the outside world to make you whole, for you were born whole. You are complete. The key is to remember that, reopen the doors and bind into something bigger than yourself. This is a process Frankincense loves to help you with.

Frankincense assists by sweeping away limiting thoughts that clutter your mind. The chaos of "all the things," the to-do lists, and the worries and fears that creep in. All these do is steal you from the present and send you into low-frequency, doubt-filled spirals. This potent resin from the deserts of Somalia gathers these thoughts and whisks them out of your mind, connecting you to the higher vibrations of love, knowing, and Source.

This essential oil beams a warm light to clear away even the heaviest, most depressed feelings so that you can return to what is now—to be safe and held and connected again.

It invites you to bask in the glory of all that you have accomplished and all that you have learned and all the ways you have grown. Reflecting back the radiance of your evolution, Frankincense encourages you to see your magnificence and collected wisdom. You are a child of Light, of the Universe, of God.

Questions:

Where would you like to invite in more Source energy?
How can you remind yourself to lean on Frankincense in times of worry?
What gifts and benefits have you received from your challenging times?

Living Ritual Daily:

Use Frankincense to bring healing to your life, body and mind. Place two drops on the back of your neck when you're feeling sad and somber. Add Myrrh and Sandalwood for a trinity of healing over the Head and Heart Chakras.

· · ·

When you are overwhelmed and lost in worry, ask Frankincense to soothe and calm your stimulated brain and elevate your thinking into higher realms. Rub 1 drop each Wild Orange and Frankincense into your temples and palms, take deep breaths. Hum, sing or tone until you feel a shift.

Use Frankincense in your meditations. Diffuse or apply one drop to your third-eye. Use sound healing and combine with Rose to open up to more Universal love and life force energy.

When you do your daily meditations, apply three drops to the back of your neck, Solar Plexus, and Sacral Chakra. Combine with Bergamot for Solar Plexus and Fennel for Sacral Chakra.

BONUS ESSENTIAL OIL!

As I complete this book, I'm already making notes for my next one. This will become a series of books on the Spiritual Messages of the Plants. For now I give you a bonus oil : Oregano! My gift to you! Enjoy.

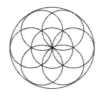

OREGANO: THE OIL OF RENEWING

May you allow yourself to be forgiven.
May you gracefully shed your skin and emerge anew.
May you enter the most sacred of places of your Heart.
May you love yourself a little bit harder.

Oregano's Message:

I am in a deep dark place within myself. I see a flicker of scaly green—something slithering and twisting, moving in and out of the blackness. Oregano comes to me as an Earth Fire Serpent.

She has invited me inside the realm in which she resides. She leads me to the entrance of deeper levels of myself. She knows me, intimately, for she has watched me, and you, walk this Earth for every incarnation. She is a story-keeper— she remembers and therefore has the power to erase and forget stories, too. She is pleased to share her gifts with us.

Oregano moves through the stagnant places in your body and mind, eating away at the debris left there. She blows her hot breath on the old and dusty. She burrows deeper and deeper, making way for the light to shine in places that have long been dark.

Oregano uncovers your lost and hidden dreams, desires and, especially, the expectations you have secretly held onto. Oregano is a master at unknotting these tangled threads. The work is tireless for her. She frees each string so that you may untangle yourself from the influence of the expectations that limit your reality. She hands them back and urges you to weave a new experience.

She knows others have failed and hurt you. She saw when you built that wall around your heart. She saw when you shielded yourself from others. And a tear rolls down her cheek, for she knows the huge cost of your fortress—it keeps out the pain, and also the pleasure, joy and happiness. Allow her to take down the wall and lift those heavy bricks. Your beautiful fortress is also a dungeon.

This Plant Ally is the goddess of dismemberment and will help you dis-member to remember and dismantle to re-mantle. She practices the art of re-alignment so that light, harmony and healing can recon-struct from the inside out.

Mighty Oregano extracts low vibrations and negative self-talk. She eliminates the echo of disapproving and false messages you've taken in from others. She has the ability to dissolve old history and old memo-ries, making space for you to create new ones.

Oregano tears down illusion. She is a truth seeker and a truth-revealer. Ask her to unveil hidden truths and false façades and call on her to transform a stagnant relationship. Non-attachment is in her magic. She brings you to an elevated perspective, so you can untangle from the details—and relinquish, release, renew.

She also tells me that we are *done* with the Karmic lessons of learning. Just like when you were a kid and it was time for the training wheels to come off your bike, now is the time to ascend beyond the confines of the endlessly-spinning Karmic wheel. Oregano can help clear not only the Karma you've collected during your time on earth, but also the Karmic baggage of your lineage and all the ways it affects you. The Earth Fire Serpent is emerging to help lift you out of this cycle. Oregano says, *"You have paid your dues. It's time to move on!"*

This pungent essential oil opens the sacred realms for your awakening. She hands over the keys to the holy places within you—where you can reflect, rebirth, and remember your essences. She bows her head as you walk through the once-locked chambers of your heart and whispers your name: *"I see you. I honor you. I love you, Earth Child."*

Questions

What story are you ready to shed?
What truth do you want revealed?
What illusions keep you comfortable?
What Karma are you ready to release?

Living Ritual Daily

Are you stuck in a story? A pattern? A cycle? Allow this essential oil to dissolve it. Use it with intention. Ask Oregano to eat away at that old story, as well as the old memory of it. Place 2 drops of this oil diluted on the bottoms of each foot. Ask to walk into a world where the new story is already so.

What would you like to leave behind? As you breathe in this oil, Oregano asks you to *Name it. Forgive it. Thank it. Bless it.* Combine 1 drop of Oregano with 3 drops of Siberian Fir and 2 drops of Pink Pepper to create a powerful diffuser blend. Write these things on a piece of paper. Safely using an outdoor fire, fireplace or candle, burn what you have written.

Place a diluted blend of Oregano and Tangerine up and down your spine to clear out the debris of old Karma. This will lift old agreements and break old declarations. Repeat: "I am sovereign. Let me be, Unbounded, Unbounded. I am free."

Use Oregano to shield yourself from others' attachments and to cut cords. This can also work in reverse. Cut the cords you have consciously or unconsciously created. Use this oil daily to keep you and others sovereign. Blend 3 drops of Oregano and 8 drops of Protective Blend in a 10 ml bottle. Rub into your belly, above and below the navel.

AN INVITATION TO WORK WITH AMBER JANE ARQUETTE

The truth is we can't do big work alone. We are too sneaky smart for our own good.

Amber Jane combines essential oil plant medicine and energy healing sessions to burst you out of stuck places and help you claim your life force energy, your wellness and your emotional balance - so that nothing holds you back!

Her 90-day program gives you 1:1 access to her, bottles of essential oils, personalized healing protocols, healing sessions and other tools to make powerful shifts in your life.

Find all the details here:
www.amberjanehealing.com

Already have oils and want to work with her? This 90 day program includes you too.

Your time is now!

BLENDS RECIPES

Breathing Blend: Laurel Leaf, Eucalyptus Leaf, Peppermint Plant, Melaleuca Leaf, Lemon Peel, Cardamom Seed, Ravintsara Leaf, Ravensara Leaf.

Digestive Blend: Anise Seed, Peppermint Plant, Ginger Rhizome/Root, Caraway Seed, Coriander Seed, Tarragon Plant, and Fennel Seed.

Massage Blend: Cypress Plant, Peppermint Plant, Marjoram Leaf, Basil Leaf, Grapefruit Peel, Lavender Flower.

Protecting Blend: Wild Orange Peel, Clove Bud, Cinnamon Leaf, Cinnamon Bark, Eucalyptus Leaf, and Rosemary Leaf/Flower.

Shielding Blend: Ylang Ylang Flower, Tamanu Seed, Nootka Wood, Cedarwood Wood, Catnip Plant, Lemon Eucalyptus Leaf, Litsea Fruit, Vanilla Bean Absolute, Arborvitae Wood.

Soothing Blend: Wintergreen, Camphor, Peppermint, Ylang Ylang, Helichrysum, Blue Tansy, Blue Chamomile, and Osmanthus.

CREATING SPIRITUAL SAFETY

Throughout my life and all the New Age, spiritual teachings and healings, ceremonies and circles I have experience, not many have spoken to Spiritual Safety. This is so important. Just as you would teach a child to bundle up before going out to the snow, I believe navigating the unseen realm is just as important.

We live in what is known as the middle world. We have joy and sorrow, pain and pleasure, good intentions, not so good intentions and even subconscious intentions, *and* so does the Spirit world. Just as we have a variety of people there are a variety of spiritual beings on this planet and in this dimension. Lets enter this environment with awareness, safety and preparedness just as we would in the brisk and freezing cold.

"The Lakota people believe we are born with 408 Allies."
- Jan Engle-Smith

"Lets start calling them in!"
-Amber Jane Arquette

I'll start with Angels for they seem to be most familiar to many. Angels are assigned to care and look out for you. They are your physical safe guards. And when you call on them they have more freedom to step in and do so. They love to help you and are just waiting in the wings for you to ask. Call on them daily to look over you. Call on them for specific help and to keep you safe. Call on them when you feel unsafe. I call on them every time I get into the car! When entering ritual or ceremony ask them to surround you while you do your work.

Allies are the ones who are specific to you. If you are clearing a room, blessing a friend, praying or pulling Oracle cards. Your Allies are the ones whom often give you messages and taps on the shoulders. Call on your benevolent Allies to guide you with their wisdom and strengths.

Guide can be a broad term to give a name to the unseen or unknown. They can sometimes be Upper World Teachers or Lower World Animals/Nature Spirits. Call on your benevolent and compassionate ones to guide your way, intuition and set you up for success. In sacred work call on them to lend their gifts and wisdom.

Benevolent Ancestors, I say benevolent because those are the ones I suggest to work with. These loving ones are invested in your well being. They want to see you happy and prosperous. Call on the higher consciousness of your beloved Ancestors to gain access to the knowledge they have collected and access to your DNA and lineage history. You can even use one of the protocols with the intention of healing your Ancestral line! Call them in to help navigate new places or experiences. I might mention here to ask for their advice to END, so you are not continuously given advice or nudges - they still might have their own agendas.

. . .

Whenever I feel I need to, and especially at the start of the day, I ask to merge with my True Self. I call to my Angels for protection and my benevolent compassionate loving Guides and Allies to help me throughout my day.

In Ritual I raise a voice to the benevolent energies of the directions, elements and the protecting spirits. I ask them to stand at the four corners of myself, others (if present) and the four corners of the room I am in. This is Spiritual Safety. We should all have the freedom and protection to create and work in sacred space. I hope knowing these simple basics will keep you safe and sovereign and not out in the cold, so to say!

May this create a most beautiful, pure and radiant space for you to empower and transform your life when you are Living Ritual Daily.

INDEX

* * *

Amber Jane Arquette
www.AmberJaneHealing.com
Portland, Oregon

SHARE YOUR JOURNEY WITH US ON-LINE

I would love to hear from you! Use the hashtag #plantwisdom #amberjanehealing #livingritualdaily

NOTES

Made in the USA
Lexington, KY
20 September 2019

Take a Guess

Written by Terry Briggs
Illustrated by Michael Carroll

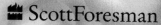
ScottForesman
A Division of HarperCollins*Publishers*

What's in the box?

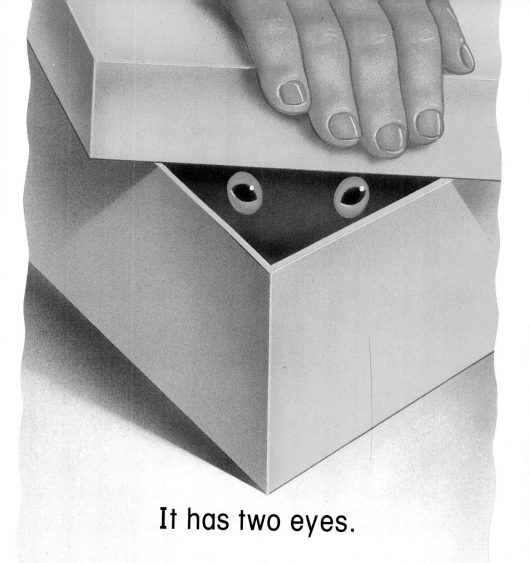

It has two eyes.

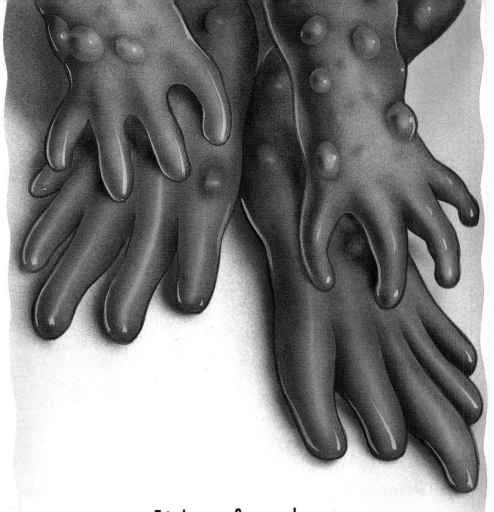

It has four legs.

It has bumps.

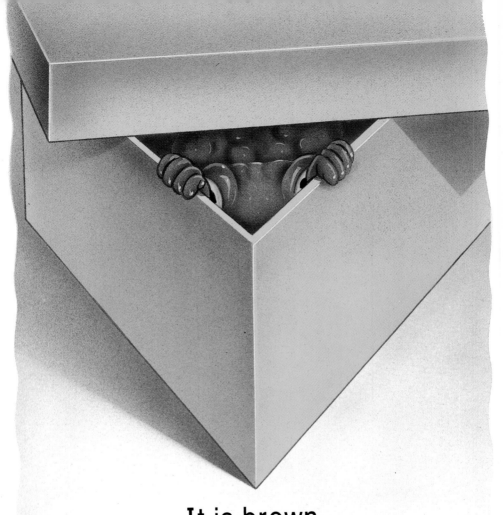

It is brown.

It hops.
Take a guess.

Croak! Croak!